Can
Science
Solve?

The Mystery
of
Black Holes

Chris Oxlade

Heinemann Library
Chicago, Illinois

Designed by **AMR**
Illustrations by Art Construction and Margaret Payne at AMR
Printed in China

04
10 9 8 7 6 5

Library of Congress Cataloging-in-Publication Data

Oxlade, Chris.
        The mystery of black holes / Chris Oxlade.
            p. cm. – (Can science solve?)
        Includes bibliographical references and index.
        Summary: Explores the phenomenon of black holes, explains why
astronomers think they exist, what causes them, what they are like
inside, and the search to find black holes in space.
        ISBN 1-57572-808-7 (lib. bdg.)
        1. Black holes (Astronomy)—Juvenile literature. [1. Black holes
(Astronomy)] I. Title. II. Series.
        QB843.B55O88 1999
        523.8'875—DC21   99-17399
                                                                        CIP

Acknowledgments

The Publishers would like to thank the following for permission to reproduce
photographs:

Bildarchiv Preussischer Kulturbesitz, p. 12; Mary Evans Picture Library, p. 10; Ronald
Grant Archive, p. 18; Science Photo Library, p. 6; D. Besford, p. 26; Celestial Image
Co., p. 14; T. Craddock, p. 17; F. Evelegh, p. 5; D. Hardy, pp. l5, 24; M. Kulyk, p. 4;
Library of Congress, p.11; NASA, pp. 6, 20; D. Nunuk, p. 22; Royal Observatory,
Edinburgh, p. 29; Dr. S. Shostak, p. 21; Space Telescope Science Institute/NASA,
pp. 25, 27.

Cover photograph reproduced with permission of Dr. S. Shostak, Science
Photo Library.

Every effort has been made to contact copyright holders of any material
reproduced in this book. Any omissions will be rectified in subsequent printings
if notice is given to the Publisher.

Some words are shown in bold, **like this**. You can find
out what they mean by looking in the Glossary.

Contents

Unsolved Mysteries

For centuries, people have been puzzled and fascinated by mysterious places, creatures, and events. Why have ships and planes vanished without a trace when crossing the Bermuda Triangle? Are some houses really haunted by ghosts? Does the Abominable Snowman actually exist? What secrets are held by a black hole?

These mysteries have baffled scientists who have spent years trying to find the answers. But how far can science go? Can science explain the seemingly unexplainable, or are there mysteries that science simply cannot solve? Read on and decide for yourself.

This book tells about the mystery of black holes. It discusses the theories of their cause. It examines the search for their existence. It asks if science can account for the evidence of black holes in space.

In billions of years, the universe could end as all the matter in it flows into a colossal, unseen black hole.

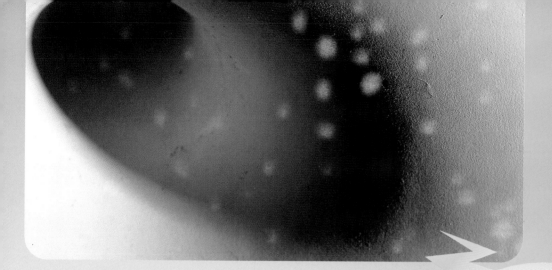

What is a black hole?

A black hole is a place in space where **gravity** is so super strong that nothing can escape it—not even light. When scientists call a black hole a giant cosmic **vacuum,** they do not mean it sucks up anything that comes near it. However, anything passing close to a black hole will be affected by its strong gravitational pull.

Astronomers think that events become very strange both near and inside black holes. The known world ceases to exist, time slows down, space is warped, and the accepted laws of physics no longer apply. No one could go into a mysterious black hole to investigate, because they would never return.

In most great mysteries, such as UFOs (unidentified flying objects), science tries to explain the strange things that people claim to have seen. In the case of black holes, however, things are the other way around. Scientists predicted the existence of black holes long before there was any real evidence that they existed. In fact, the very nature of black holes means they cannot be seen to be believed!

How did astronomers come to predict the existence of such mysterious things? What can science do to prove that black holes really exist?

Gravity, Light, and Motion

An explanation of what **astronomers** think happens in black holes needs some knowledge of **astrophysics.** Astrophysics is the branch of astronomy that describes the physical characteristics of things in the universe. Two of the characteristics that astrophysicists study are **gravity** and light. What is gravity? How does it make things move? How does light travel?

About gravity

Gravity is a **force** that attracts (pulls together) every object that has mass towards every other object. Mass is the amount of matter an object, or body, contains. The amount of gravitational pull between two bodies depends on the mass of the two bodies and the distance between them. The greater the masses, the greater the force. The further the distance between them, the smaller the force. The amount of gravitational pull between bodies is very tiny unless one of the bodies is very massive, such as a planet.

This is called the Law of Universal Gravitation. It was first written by the English scientist Sir Isaac Newton (1642–1727). This law of gravity explains how the gravitational pull between bodies causes the planets to **orbit** the sun.

Sir Isaac Newton developed theories in mathematics and physics that scientists use today.

A body has a **gravitational field** around it. Any other object in the field experiences a pull from the body, which pulls the object towards it.

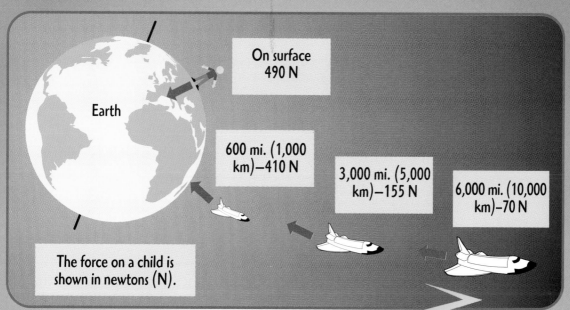

On surface
490 N

Earth

600 mi. (1,000 km)—410 N

3,000 mi. (5,000 km)—155 N

6,000 mi. (10,000 km)—70 N

The force on a child is shown in newtons (N).

The nature of light

Light travels in waves of particles called photons. Eyes detect light. Some objects, such as stars, can be seen because they make light. Other objects, such as planets or this book, can be seen because light bounces off them.

As you move away from Earth, the force with which you are pulled toward Earth decreases.

Light travels very fast. In the **vacuum** of space, the speed of light is 186,282 miles (300,000 kilometers) per second. Its speed decreases when it passes through substances, such as air and glass.

Mass and weight

Mass and weight are often confused. In physics, the mass of an object is the amount of matter in it. Mass is measured in kilograms (kg). Weight is the pull of gravity on an object. Weight is a force. It is measured by both the mass and gravity. It is measured in units called newtons (N). The mass of an object is always the same, but its weight can change.

Early Theories

Black holes are sometimes featured in science-fiction movies and might be thought of as a 20th-century invention. But ideas about strange objects that were different from the stars and planets that **astronomers** could see were actually put forward hundreds of years ago.

Light and gravity

When Sir Isaac Newton devised his Law of Universal Gravitation, he also suggested that light was subjected to the pull of **gravity**. On Earth, light always travels in a straight line, unless it hits an object. But light does bend as it passes close to bodies with very strong **gravitational fields**, such as very massive stars. This shows that the things we take for granted on Earth do not necessarily apply when super strong gravity is at work.

Stars appear to change position when their light passes close to another star on its way to Earth.

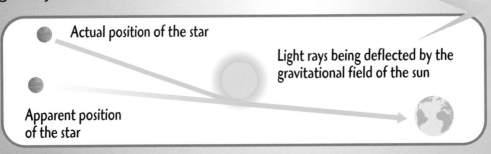

Actual position of the star

Light rays being deflected by the gravitational field of the sun

Apparent position of the star

Dark stars

Pierre Laplace (1749–1827), a French mathematician and astronomer, was one of the first people to suggest that black holes could exist. As an expert on celestial mechanics, he knew how the planets and moons move around the sun. In his book, *Exposition of the System of the World*, published in 1795, Laplace made an amazing prediction.

Laplace realized that if a star were massive enough, its escape velocity (see below) would be greater than the speed of light. So he calculated how big a star would have to be, if it had the same overall **density** as Earth, to have an escape velocity equal to the speed of light. He calculated that the star would have to be 250 times the **diameter** of the sun. Laplace predicted that a star of this size would have such an enormous gravitational pull that light particles would never leave its surface. The star would be invisible.

Escape velocity

Imagine throwing a ball straight up. The Earth's gravity would gradually slow it down and make it fall back to Earth. But if a ball was thrown upward fast enough, gravity would not be able to stop it escaping into space. The minimum speed needed for this to happen is called escape velocity. On Earth, escape velocity is 25,000 miles (40,000 kilometers) per hour.

*Space rockets must accelerate to a minimum of 17,000 miles (27,000 kilometers) per hour to stay in **orbit** around Earth. They must travel faster to escape from Earth.*

Changing the Rules

There are two important differences between Laplace's idea of a dark star and the modern idea of a black hole. The differences are due to two important discoveries of modern **astrophysics**. The first discovery is that nothing can travel faster than light. This means that if light cannot escape from a massive star, nothing can. This also means that a dark star is a hole, because nothing that is pulled in by the star's **gravity** can ever escape. The second difference is that Laplace used Newton's laws of gravity as the basis of his work. Modern astrophysics says that these laws do not work in and around black holes.

Albert Einstein is shown here at the age of 42. His Special Theory of Relativity was published when he was just 26.

Everything is relative

The person who thought about and predicted these differences was perhaps the most famous scientist of all time, Albert Einstein (1879–1955). In his General Theory of Relativity, Einstein put forward a new theory about the size of gravitational **forces**. Newton's and Einstein's theories give almost exactly the same answer on Earth, where the **gravitational field** is quite weak, but their theories are very different for super strong gravity. Einstein showed that Newton's laws did not work in black holes.

More relativity

Einstein made other predictions in his General Theory of Relativity. He said that in super strong gravitational fields, time passes more slowly than it does outside the field. And, as gravity becomes **infinitely** strong, time actually slows to a stop. He also said that all the laws of **geometry** would no longer be true because three-dimensional space would be changed and distorted. For example, the geometry rule that the area of a square is equal to its length multiplied by its width would not be true in super strong gravity.

Einstein and his wife, Elsa, visited America in 1930. Einstein later moved to the United States, where he worked on the nuclear bomb program and then later campaigned for nuclear disarmament.

Einstein's other great theory, the Special Theory of Relativity, predicted that the passing of time and the measurement of distance change as movement becomes faster and faster. The effects of this become noticeable only as the speed of light is approached. This would have consequences for black holes, since objects that fall into black holes would begin to go as fast as the speed of light.

A Theoretical Black Hole

Armed with Einstein's theories, the German **astronomer** Karl Schwarzschild (1873–1916) developed the idea of the black hole as we know it today. He did not call it a black hole. This term was first used in the late 1960s by the American physicist John Wheeler. Before Wheeler, they were called "frozen stars."

Gravitational radius

The French mathematician Pierre Laplace used Newton's laws to calculate the size of a body that would stop light from escaping. Karl Schwarzschild calculated at what distance from the center of a body the escape velocity would be the speed of light. He used Einstein's relativity theory. Remember that the **force** of **gravity** between two objects gets greater and greater as the objects get closer together. At a certain distance from a body, the gravity becomes so great that the escape velocity becomes greater than the speed of light.

Karl Schwarzschild published his first scientific paper at the age of 16 and became a professor of astronomy at age 28.

Schwarzschild calculated the relationship between this distance from a body's center and the mass of the body. This distance is known as the **gravitational radius** or Schwarzschild **radius**.

For bodies such as planets and stars, Schwarzschild's radius is much smaller than the body. For example, for Earth, it is less than one half of an inch (one centimeter), and it is about one and a half miles (two and a half kilometers) for the sun.

Schwarzschild's theory was that a black hole was formed if the gravitational radius of a body was larger than its actual radius. This means a body would have to be squeezed into an extremely tiny space. For example, Earth would have to be squashed to the size of a pea for it to become a black hole.

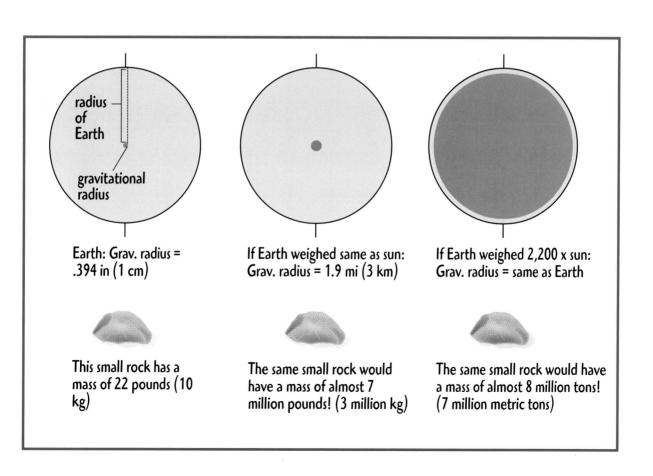

radius of Earth

gravitational radius

Earth: Grav. radius = .394 in (1 cm)

If Earth weighed same as sun: Grav. radius = 1.9 mi (3 km)

If Earth weighed 2,200 x sun: Grav. radius = same as Earth

This small rock has a mass of 22 pounds (10 kg)

The same small rock would have a mass of almost 7 million pounds! (3 million kg)

The same small rock would have a mass of almost 8 million tons! (7 million metric tons)

How Are Black Holes Formed?

Karl Schwarzschild predicted that a black hole would be formed when a massive star stopped shining and collapsed in on itself. The **gravity** would be so large that the material would become more and more dense, making the gravity still stronger. Gravity would eventually become so great that the star would keep collapsing past its **gravitational radius**. Once past this point, nothing would stop the star collapsing until nothing was left except a **gravitational field**! In 1939, American **astrophysicists** Robert Oppenheimer and Hartland Snyder used mathematics to show that this collapse would happen.

The life of a star

Before looking at how a star collapses to become a black hole, let's look at its life. Stars are formed inside vast clouds of gas and dust called **nebulae**. Over billions of years, gravity causes the gas and dust to drift together to form clumps called protostars. Each protostar shrinks until its center becomes so dense that nuclear reactions begin inside it, and it starts to shine.

The Orion nebula, a huge cloud of gas and dust, is lit by the light of nearby stars.

14

Stars come in different sizes. The sun is a pretty average star, which glows yellow. Larger stars glow blue or white because they are hotter, but they don't shine for as long. Smaller stars glow orange or red. They are cooler and last longer.

After thousands of millions of years, the nuclear reactions in the sun will stop. Gravity will then squeeze the core, creating heat that will make the outer layers swell, swallowing Earth. The outer layers will drift into space, leaving a planet-sized star called a white dwarf.

Supernovas and neutron stars

Stars that are more then ten times more massive than the sun end their lives in a different way. The core squeezes itself so much that there is a huge explosion called a supernova. Sometimes the heavy core turns into something called a neutron star, which is just a short distance across. The material of a neutron star is very dense. A piece of it the size of a grain of sand weighs a million tons! If the core is twice as heavy as the sun, it keeps collapsing and becomes a black hole.

A supernova illuminates clouds of dust and gas in space in this artist's drawing.

Is a Black Hole Really a Hole?

A black hole is not a solid object, like a planet, but it is shaped like a sphere. **Astronomers** think that at the center of a black hole there is a very strange object indeed. It is a single point in space with **infinite density** called a **singularity**. The mass is not infinite, but the density is, because the point has no size.

Unfortunately, because nothing can escape from the black hole, we can't see whether this is true or not! If the singularity theory is correct, it means that when a massive star collapses, all the material in it disappears into the singularity. The center of a black hole is not really a hole; nor is it a tunnel to anywhere else in the universe.

The event horizon

A black hole has no surface. It begins at the **gravitational radius**. The sphere at the gravitational radius is called the **event horizon**. The event horizon is the point of no return. Anything that crosses it can never come back. Outside the event horizon is a region called the ergosphere. Anything in the ergosphere rotates with the black hole, but also has the possibility of escaping.

Dips and holes

Einstein imagined space as a sheet of rubber material that represents space and time. This sheet has dents in it created by the **gravity** of bodies. A planet makes a tiny dent in the surface, and a star makes a much greater dent. Einstein imagined that things could escape from the dips of a dent, but never from the funnel created by a black hole.

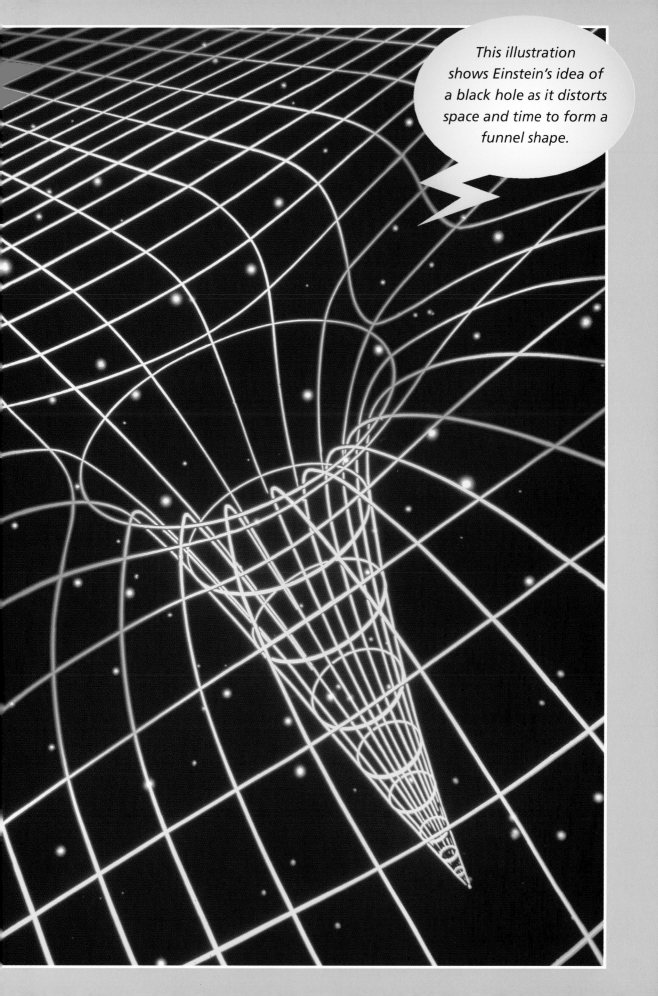

Into a Black Hole

A commonly held belief, probably created by science fiction movies, is that a black hole "sucks" in everything around it with its massive **gravity**. This is not what happens. A black hole's gravity will cause a passing object that is a long distance away to change its direction, but continue its path. Objects can **orbit** a black hole just as Earth orbits the sun. Only objects that pass very close to or aim straight for a black hole disappear into it.

Many false ideas about what happens in black holes come from science fiction movies and TV programs, such as Star Trek.

Gravitational tides

The farther one body gets from the center of another body, the weaker the **gravitational field** is. For example, when you stand on Earth's surface, the field is stronger at your feet than at your head. This difference in strength is called a gravitational tide. It tries to stretch you with a **force** called tidal force. This force is not noticed on Earth, because it is extremely small. But on the edge of a black hole, tidal force is much bigger.

Over the horizon

What would happen if a spacecraft flew toward a black hole? Of course, this would not be a wise flight plan! The gravity of the black hole would accelerate the spacecraft to faster and faster speeds. By the time it reached the **event horizon,** it would be traveling at the speed of light. Once over the event horizon, it would cease to exist. It would become part of the hole's **singularity** within a millionth of a second.

But before reaching the event horizon, the spacecraft and its passengers would have been pulled apart by tidal forces of the massively strong gravitational field. Even the very small particles of atoms would be ripped apart. Strangely, the bigger the black hole, the smaller the tidal forces. So a spacecraft would survive longer in a very large black hole, but only until it crossed the event horizon.

Stranger still would be the experience of watching a person going into a black hole. Einstein's laws say that time slows down in strong fields. But, it does not slow down for the person going into the black hole; it only slows down for the person outside the field. This means that for the person watching outside of the horizon, it would take forever for the person entering the black hole to reach the event horizon!

19

Searching for Black Holes

So far in this book, everything has been theory. These theories were developed before the middle of the twentieth century, before anyone had even looked for a real black hole in space. In fact, it was not until the 1960s that **astronomers** began to scientifically search for black holes. Even then, many astronomers found it hard to accept the existence of black holes, because the theory was so far removed from the world of astronomy that they understood. Some astronomers refused to discuss black holes. Others said that even if black holes did exist, they would be impossible to find.

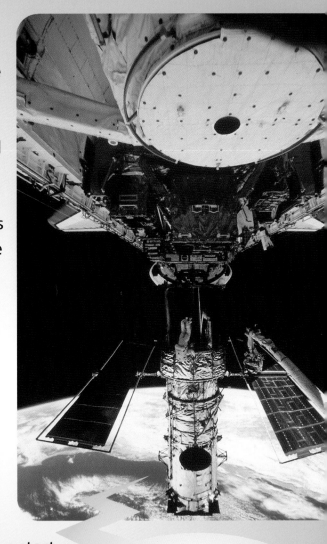

*The Hubble Space Telescope was launched in 1990. It **orbits** Earth and can give much better images of space than any telescope on Earth.*

Spotting black holes

Black holes are not easy to find. For a start, they are black! No light or anything else comes out of them. This makes them completely invisible to a telescope. Second, in astronomical terms, they are very, very small. For example, a black hole formed by the collapse of a giant star would have an **event horizon** of perhaps just 18 miles (30 kilometers) across. Third, astronomers realized that if black holes were made from massive stars, then the nearest ones would be dozens of light years away. A light year is the distance light travels in a year. It is about 6 trillion miles (10 trillion kilometers). Even the most powerful telescopes could not pick out an object so small at such a huge distance. It would be like trying to see a grain of sand on the moon from Earth.

The only way to find a black hole is to look for evidence of its effect on other bodies in the space around it. These effects should be quite large because of the immensely strong **gravity** around the black hole.

Binary stars

The first approach astronomers took was to look for black holes in binary star systems. A binary system is made up of two stars close together that orbit around each other. Most stars in the universe are in binary systems. Astronomers realized that if they saw a single star moving as if it was in a binary system, then its companion could be a black hole. Astronomers in the former **USSR** and in the United States found many cases that could be black holes, but this was not proof. The other body could be another type of dead star, such as a neutron star.

This is an artist's impression of how a binary star system containing a black hole might look.

X-ray Proof

After failing to find a definite black hole in a binary star system, **astronomers** decided to look into gas **nebulae**. They realized that the gas and dust of a nebula could fall into a black hole. If it did, it would accelerate to a high speed and be heated to extremely high temperatures. The falling nebula would give out not just light, but other types of **electromagnetic radiation**, such as radio waves, too. Using radio telescopes, astronomers scanned likely nebulae looking for radio waves. Unfortunately, this search produced nothing. Perhaps there were black holes where they were looking, but the amount of gas and dust going into them was so small that the radio waves were too weak to detect.

X-ray binaries

Astronomers did not give up. In 1966, they looked again at binary stars. They realized that if one of the stars in a binary star pair was a black hole, and, if the other star and the black hole were close together, then there would be a huge gravitational pull. They could expect to see the black hole pulling gas from the outer layers of the star into the hole.

Radio telescopes are used to detect radio waves coming from space. The huge dishes collect the weak waves and concentrate them on sensors.

The gas from the star would spiral at enormous speed around the hole before falling into it. This would create immense heat and **X-rays**. But in order to detect the X-rays, astronomers had to launch a special telescope into space.

There was another problem to be solved, too. Stars called **pulsars** also create X-rays. An X-ray-producing binary star could either contain a pulsar or a black hole. If the motion of the binary stars told astronomers that the dark star had a mass greater than twice that of the Sun, then they had probably found a black hole, rather than a pulsar.

A pulsar acts like a lighthouse. It sends out two beams of radiation as it spins around.

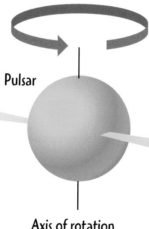

Pulsar

Beam of radiation from pulsar

On Earth, we can detect a pulse of radiation each time a beam sweeps by.

Axis of rotation

A pulsar is a spinning neutron star. It is sometimes formed after the collapse of a star.

X-ray astronomy

Unlike light, X-rays cannot get through Earth's atmosphere. So, in order to look for X-rays from space, it was necessary to launch a special telescope into orbit around Earth. UHURU, the first satellite whose only mission was X-ray astronomy, was launched from Kenya, Africa, in 1970. It soon found the first X-ray binaries.

Case Studies

Cygnus X-1

The first candidate for a black hole was found in 1971. It was in the **constellation** of Cygnus. The source of the **X-rays** in the constellation is called Cygnus X-1, and it is about 6,000 light years from Earth. At the source is a blue **supergiant star**. It is 20 times more massive than Earth's sun. Every five and a half days, this supergiant star makes an **orbit** of its binary companion. The companion is invisible, but ten times more massive than the Sun. Because it is massive and a source of X-rays, **astronomers** believe it is a black hole formed by a collapsed supergiant star.

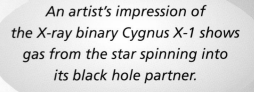

An artist's impression of the X-ray binary Cygnus X-1 shows gas from the star spinning into its black hole partner.

Gas that is pulled from the supergiant star does not go straight into this black hole. Instead, it travels in a huge spiral that orbits the black hole. The gas forms a disk around the hole. Friction between the layers of the disk makes the gas extremely hot. The friction also makes the inner layers gradually slow down and fall into the hole.

Since Cygnus X-1 was discovered, several other possible black holes have been found. Most stars in our **galaxy,** which is called the Milky Way, are in binary systems. Millions of them are supergiants. Therefore, it is possible that there are millions of black holes in our own Milky Way.

M87 galaxy

Collapsed and dying stars might not be the only source of black holes. Many galaxies have extremely active centers that give out strong X-rays and radio waves. The source of these waves could be a massive black hole big enough to rip apart any stars that come within its reach.

In 1994, the Hubble Space Telescope photographed the M87 galaxy. The images showed strong activity in its center that was far greater than normal star activity. At its center is thought to be a supermassive black hole.

Measurements of the speed of gases in the center of the Milky Way show that there is probably a massive black hole there, too. Black holes could also account for the brightness of **quasars,** which are objects brighter than stars in our galaxy, but are thousands of millions of light years away. It is thought that many large galaxies may have a black hole in the center.

Although unseen, there may be a black hole at the center of this galaxy, which is similar to M87. The dark, oval shape is gas and dust swirling into the hole.

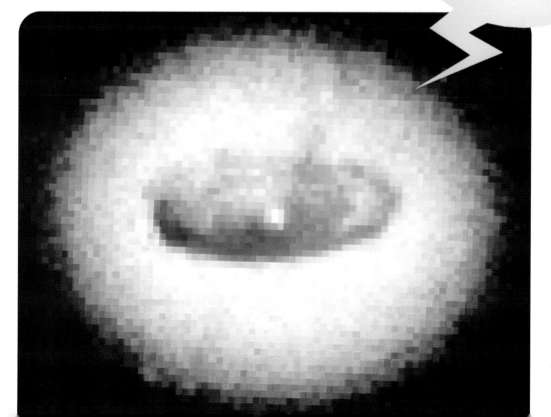

New Ideas

Theory predicts that black holes are formed by the collapse of massive stars and are often at the centers of **galaxies**. Theory also says that nothing can escape from a black hole. This must also mean that black holes can never be destroyed. Can this be true? English physicist Stephen Hawking (b. 1942) thinks not. He has many new theories about the universe.

Professor Stephen Hawking continues his research into relativity and black holes despite having a degenerative disease that affects his movement and speech.

Early black holes

Hawking suggests that many small black holes were formed during the **Big Bang**, when most scientists think the universe was born. The Big Bang was an unimaginably enormous explosion. These black holes could not have been formed by the collapse of stars, because there were no stars then. These black holes would now be undetectable. This is because all the matter around them, such as nearby stars and gas, would have fallen in, and **X-ray emissions** would have stopped.

Hawking also suggests that some of the black holes made in the early moments of the universe were mini-black holes, perhaps no larger than a house. These would gradually have dispersed all their energy and finally disappeared.

Worm holes

Hawking thinks that the **singularity** theory, that there is a single point with **infinite density** at a black hole's center, may not be correct. Instead of the singularity at the center, Hawking says there is a hole that he calls a worm hole. Worm holes, he says, lead into another universe, completely separate from our own.

Black holes and the universe

The study of black holes could help **astronomers** to work out information about how the universe works, how it began, and what might happen in the future. There may be similarities between what happens at the singularity in a black hole and what happened during the Big Bang. They may find that the entire universe was born from a supermassive black hole!

*At the bright center of this photograph is a **quasar**, a superbright, distant galaxy that emits strong radio waves. Perhaps the quasar has a massive black hole at its center.*

In Conclusion

The mystery surrounding black holes is strange, because the existence of black holes was predicted long before **astronomers** could find any real evidence.

Now some evidence has been found. So far, the evidence matches the theories, so it seems to prove that black holes do exist. But the proof is inconclusive because nobody has ever been or ever will be in a black hole. Nor will information ever be sent back to Earth from a black hole, because radio signals would not escape its **gravity!**

What happens inside a black hole is still a mystery. We have to rely on theory because we can never see inside. And just because theories about the effects of black holes on their surrounding space seem to have come true, it does not mean that theories about what happens inside are true.

Predictions about what happens in black holes are hard to comprehend. But perhaps in time, with space exploration, improved scientific instruments, and the help of great scientific minds, we will come to better understand these mysterious black holes.

The bright spot at the bottom right of this photograph is a supernova, an exploding star. It might leave another black hole in the universe.

What do you think?

Now that you have read about the theories concerning black holes and the search for them, can you draw any conclusions? Do you feel that you can believe the theories, even though they predict bizarre events? Do you accept Einstein's ideas? Or Hawking's ideas? Do you have any theories of your own? Is the evidence for black holes strong enough to conclude that they definitely exist?

Try to keep an open mind. Remember, if scientists throughout history had not investigated things that appeared at first strange or mysterious, many important scientific discoveries would never have been made.

Glossary

astronomer scientist who studies space and the objects in space

astrophysics branch of astronomy that describes the physical characteristics of things in the universe, such as brightness, size, temperature, and mass

Big Bang huge explosion that most astrophysicists think happened when the universe began. In theory, space did not exist before the Big Bang.

constellation group of stars that form a pattern when they are seen from the earth

density amount of matter contained in a certain space

diameter distance from one side of a circle to the other, as measured through the center

electromagnetic radiation rays or waves that are part of the electromagnetic spectrum, including light rays, radio waves, X-rays, and nuclear radiation

emissions electromagnetic radiation coming from an object

event horizon spherical surface that marks the outer edge of a black hole

force push or a pull

galaxy huge group of stars in space containing billions of stars

geometry branch of mathematics that studies points, lines, angles, and surfaces of shapes

gravitational field area around a body where other objects are affected by its gravity

gravitational radius distance from the center of a black hole to the event horizon. Anything inside the event horizon cannot escape from the black hole.

gravity force that attracts (pulls) all objects towards all other objects

infinite never ending or too big to measure

nebula (plural **nebulae**) enormous cloud of gas and dust in space

orbit path an object, such as a moon or satellite, takes as it moves around a star or a planet

pulsar neutron star (the remains of a giant star) that rotates, sending out radio waves and X-rays

quasar body larger than a star, but smaller than a galaxy, which gives off powerful light and radio waves.

radius distance from the center to the outside of a circle. The radius of a circle is equal to half its diameter.

singularity point at the center of a black hole that has infinite density, but no size

supergiant star brightest known type of star

USSR former Soviet Union. It has divided into separate countries, including Russia and the Ukraine.

vacuum place where there is nothing, not even air. The regions between stars and planets are a vacuum.

X-ray type of electromagnetic radiation that has a very short wave length

More Books to Read

Sipiera, Paul P. *Black Holes.* Danbury, Conn.: The Children's Press, 1997.

Couper, Heather, and Nigel Henbest. *Black Holes: A Journey to the Heart of a Black Hole.* New York: DK Publishing, Inc., 1996.

Steele, Philip. *Black Holes & Other Space Phenomena.* New York: Larousse Kingfisher Chambers, Inc., 1995.

Index